THE U.S. SUPREME COURT

by Amy Kortuem

PEBBLE
a capstone imprint

Pebble Explore is published by Pebble, an imprint of Capstone.
1710 Roe Crest Drive
North Mankato, Minnesota 56003
www.capstonepub.com

Library of Congress Cataloging-in-Publication Data is available on the Library of Congress website.
ISBN 978-1-9771-1399-3 (hardcover)
ISBN 978-1-9771-1823-3 (paperback)
ISBN 978-1-9771-1407-5 (ebook pdf)

Summary: Describes the Supreme Court's duties, how judges are chosen, where they work, and more.

Image Credits
AP Images: Alex Brandon, 11, Dana Verkouteren, 16-17, Mark Elias, 9; Newscom: ABACAUSA.COM/Roger L. Wollenberg, 15, Everett Collection, 28 (top), KRT/Franz Jantzen, 27, MEGA/Pool via CNP, 28 (bottom), Reuters/Hyungwon Kand, 4, Reuters/Pool, 18-19, 20-21, Ron Sachs - Pool via CNP, 13, UPI/Kevin Dietsch, 25, ZUMA Press/Kevin Dietsch, 10; Shutterstock: Alexkava, 6 (middle), america365, 6 (left, right), Akugasahagy, 25 (background sky), r.classen, Cover, zimmytws, 23

Design Elements
Shutterstock: graphic stocker, Nadezhda Molkentin

Editorial Credits
Anna Butzer, editor; Cynthia Della-Rovere, designer;
Jo Miller, media researcher; Laura Manthe, production specialist

All internet sites appearing in back matter were available and accurate when this book was sent to press.

Printed and bound in China.
2489

Table of Contents

What Is the Supreme Court? 4

Who Can Be on the Supreme Court? 8

How Supreme Court Judges are Chosen . .12

What Does the Supreme Court Do? 16

Where Does the Supreme Court Work?. . 24

Did You Know? 28

Fast Facts 29

Glossary. 30

Read More. 31

Internet Sites. 31

Index. 32

Words in **bold** are in the glossary.

What Is the Supreme Court?

Sometimes people can't agree who is right. They may need someone else to decide. In sports, a referee decides. At school, a teacher might decide. At home, your parents decide. In the U.S. government, the Supreme Court has the final say.

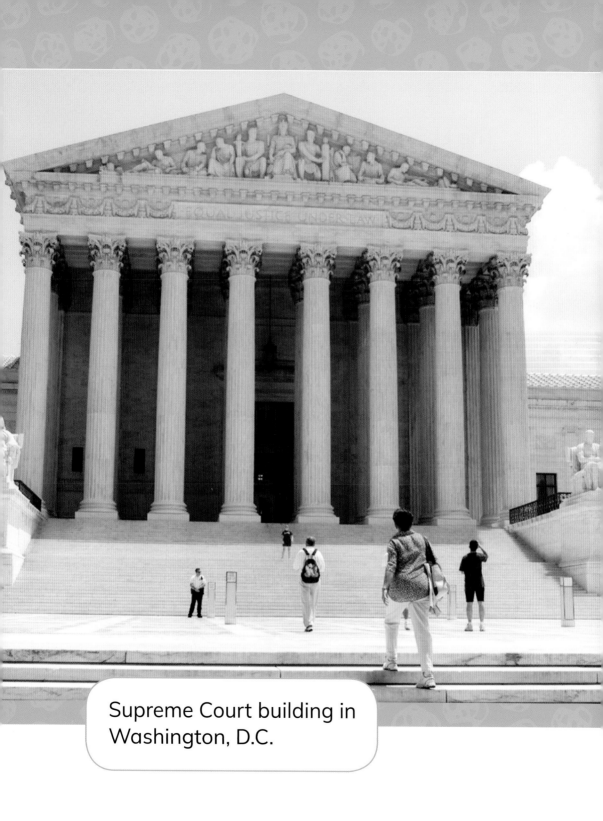

Supreme Court building in Washington, D.C.

The U.S. government has three branches, or parts. The Supreme Court is part of the **judicial branch**. The court makes **rulings** on laws and other important issues. They make sure laws follow the U.S. **Constitution**.

People go to court to decide if a law has been broken. First they go to a local or state court. Sometimes people don't like the rulings from those courts. They ask the Supreme Court to look at the case. The Supreme Court makes a final ruling.

U.S. Government

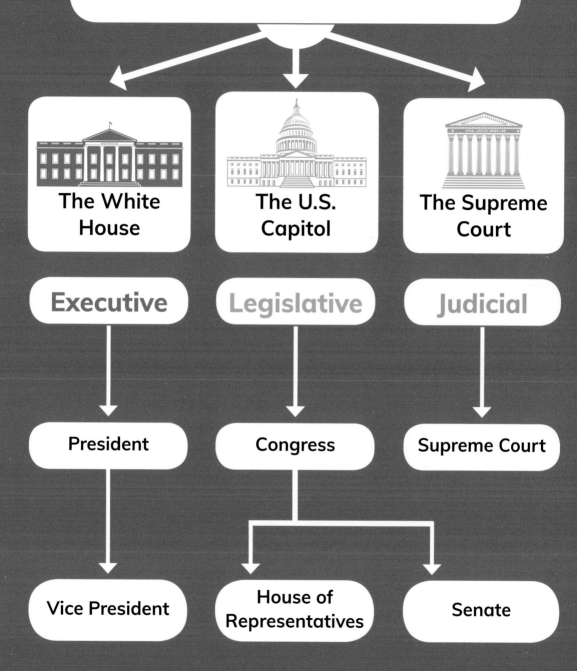

The White House — Executive — President — Vice President

The U.S. Capitol — Legislative — Congress — House of Representatives, Senate

The Supreme Court — Judicial — Supreme Court

Who Can Be on the Supreme Court?

Who can be on the Supreme Court? Anyone! But most members have some things in common.

First, they need to know about the law. All court members were lawyers. They studied laws in school. They talk about laws in court. Some members worked in government too. Many were judges before joining the Supreme Court.

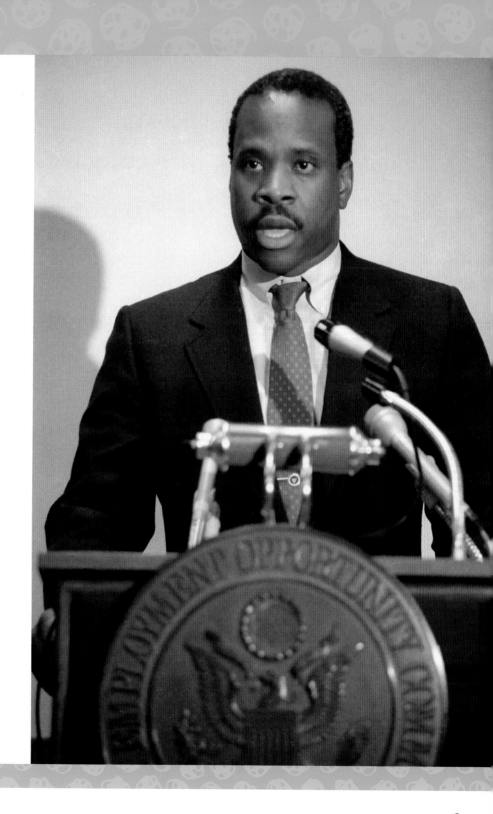

There are nine **justices** on the
Supreme Court. They serve for life
or until they want to leave.

Ruth Bader Ginsburg is the second woman to be a Supreme Court justice.

Men and women have served on the court. So have African Americans and Latinas. Some justices have been 90 years old!

How Supreme Court Judges are Chosen

Sometimes there is an opening on the court. Then the U.S. president chooses someone new. That person may join the court if he or she is approved by the **Senate**. The Senate is part of the U.S. government.

Senators ask the person questions. They ask about how the person would make decisions. Then they **vote**. If most vote "yes," the person joins the Supreme Court. If they vote "no," the president must choose someone else.

President Barack Obama (center) chose Sonia Sotomayor (right) to join the Supreme court.

The president also chooses someone to be the **Chief Justice** of the Supreme Court. Senators vote on the Chief Justice too. The Chief Justice is the leader of the Supreme Court. He or she is in charge of the court during cases.

Chief Justice John G. Roberts

What Does the Supreme Court Do?

The Supreme Court hears cases and decides what federal laws mean. They make sure federal laws follow the U.S. Constitution.

The Supreme Court will only hear the most important cases. There are cases that could change federal laws. They could change how people work or live. Each year, the Supreme Court is asked to look at almost 8,000 cases. But the court takes only about 80 of them.

The Supreme Court hears many cases each year.

Before starting work, Supreme Court justices put on long black coats. The coats are called robes. Some justices add things like collars or stripes.

Then all the justices shake hands
with each other. This shows that they
respect one another. They meet in
the Court **Chamber** to hear cases
from lawyers.

The justices listen to lawyers talk about their cases for one hour. After that, justices can ask questions. They might ask for more information.

After listening to a case, justices meet in a small room. No one else is allowed into the room.

Supreme Court justices

The Chief Justice begins the meeting. All justices talk about the case. Then they vote on the case. They don't always come to the same decision. At least five justices need to agree to make a final decision.

The Supreme Court has the power to undo decisions of lower courts. It also makes sure that laws follow the U.S. Constitution.

The U.S. Constitution guides the Supreme Court's decisions.

Where Does the Supreme Court Work?

Justices work in the Supreme Court building in Washington, D.C. This huge building is made from a white stone called **marble**. The stone came from the states of Vermont, Georgia, and Alabama.

The building has 16 round poles outside called **columns**. These are also made of marble. Large doors made of **bronze** lead into the building. These doors weigh 13,000 pounds (5.9 metric tons) each!

The Supreme Court building in Washington, D.C.

Once inside, people enter the Great Hall. This hall has statues of all the justices. The hall leads into the Court Chamber. Justices hear cases in this room. They sit in chairs on a raised step called a bench. A railing keeps the bench away from other people. Justices also have their own offices. In their offices, they study laws and cases.

Justices sit on the raised bench when hearing cases.

Did You Know?

The first African American Supreme Court justice was Thurgood Marshall in 1967.

The first woman to become a Supreme Court justice was Sandra Day O'Connor in 1981.

Fast Facts

- The Supreme Court has the final say on laws in the United States. It makes sure all laws follow the U.S. Constitution.

- There are nine justices on the Supreme Court. One is the Chief Justice.

- Supreme Court Justices serve for life or as long as they want to.

- The Supreme Court only hears cases that will make a big difference in American law.

- The president chooses the Supreme Court justices and the Chief Justice. The Senate votes "yes" or "no" on the president's choice.

Glossary

bronze (BRAHNZ)—a metal made of copper and tin; bronze has a gold-brown color

chamber (CHAYM-buhr)—a room or office used by a judge

Chief Justice (CHEEF JUHSS–tiss)—the head judge of a court of justice

column (KAH-luhm)—a tall, round pole used to support something

Constitution (kahn-stuh-TOO-shuhn)—legal document that describes the basic form of the U.S. government and the rights of citizens

judicial branch (joo-DISH-uhl BRANCH)—one of the three parts of the U.S. government

justice (JUHSS-tiss)—a judge of the Supreme Court of a country or state

marble (MAR-buhl)—a hard stone with colored patterns

ruling (ROO–ling)—a decision made by a court

Senate (SEN–it)—one of the two houses of Congress that makes laws

vote (VOHT)—a choice made by a person based on their own views

Read More

Demuth, Patricia Brennan. *What is the Constitution?* New York: Penguin Workshop, 2018.

Levy, Debbie. *I Dissent: Ruth Bader Ginsburg Makes Her Mark.* New York: Simon & Schuster Books for Young Readers, 2016.

Murray, Julie. *Supreme Court.* Minneapolis: Abdo Kids, 2018.

Internet Sites

Ben's Guide to the U.S. Government
https://bensguide.gpo.gov/

Kids Discover | Spotlight: The Supreme Court
http://www.kidsdiscover.com/spotlight/supreme-court-kids/?c_cid=1cf9ce78ac&mc_eid=369e19759c

United States Government : Judicial Branch - The Supreme Court
https://www.ducksters.com/history/us_judicial_branch.php

Index

branches of the U.S.
government, 6

cases, 14, 16, 17, 19, 20,
21, 22, 26, 29
Chief Justice, 14, 22, 29
Court Chamber, 19, 26

Great Hall, 26

judges, 8
justices, 8, 10, 11, 18, 19,
20, 21, 22, 26, 29

laws, 6, 8, 16, 17, 26, 29
lawyers, 8, 19, 20

Marshall, Thurgood, 28

O'Connor, Sandra Day, 28
offices, 26

presidents, 12, 14, 29

robes, 18
rulings, 6

Senate, 12, 29
senators, 12, 14
Supreme Court building,
24

U.S. Constitution, 6, 16,
22, 29

voting, 12, 14, 22, 29